CN00664720

kismet

jennifer lee tsai

ignitionpress

For my parents, grandparents and Chris

First published in 2019
by **ignition**press
Oxford Brookes Poetry Centre
Oxford Brookes University
OX3 0BP

Cover design: Flora Hands, Carline Creative

A CIP record for this book is available from the British Library

ISBN 978-1-9165043-5-6

Contents

The Heart asks Pleasure – first –

Emily Dickinson

Self-Portrait at Four Years Old

I am the smallest one in class / the only Oriental at a primary school in Birkenhead / At four years old, I learn to read better than a child twice my age / My first school uniform / grey cardigan knitted by an aunt / grey skirt, grey like an English sky / yellow and brown tie / shiny Clarks shoes bought by my grandfather / with money made by washing dishes in a restaurant kitchen / In the playground, I hear something I don't understand / an occasional refrain / *Chinese, Japanese, don't forget to wash your knees* / First school photo / mother reminds me to smile for the camera / I don't tell her that I never feel like smiling at school / I am learning to be silent / I am learning how to keep secrets / I am learning how to be alone / At home, I read fairy tales with my mother / Goldilocks and the Three Bears / Rapunzel / Cinderella / Sleeping Beauty / Snow White and the Seven Dwarfs / Only Snow White has black hair / Her eyes are brown, like mine / but her skin is white / What colour is my skin, mama? / I listen to nursery rhyme records on my father's turntable / *Baa-baa black sheep, have you any wool?* / *Yes sir, yes sir, three bags full* / *Humpty-Dumpty sat on the wall* / *Humpty Dumpty had a great fall* / Back from the casino, father laments my love of books / my pleas to buy them every week / because in Cantonese the word for a book sounds like the verb *to lose* / I put on my best smile for the camera

Breathing

After Song Dong

Tiananmen Square, New Year's Eve;
sub-zero temperatures.
He lies face down,
breathing gently for forty minutes.

From a distance, Mao observes.
A few policemen patrol on night watch.
The lamp posts are fitted with cameras.
This is the gate of Heavenly Peace.

A patch of frost thaws
only to freeze again when he rises.
In the morning, by the Western edge
of the Forbidden City,

he breathes over the petrified lake
in Houhai Park. Nothing gives.
The trees cast their long shadows
away from winter sunlight.

Mersey River

Listen	some shattering in the void of my form
I hear your song	borne on the cry of a seagull
the river flows	entranced by
the sea's operatic language	which beguiles
a geography of otherness	This otherness
becomes me	I swim towards the coastline
clasping mementoes	from my grandfather
a Chinese passport	papers from the Blue
Funnel Line	photographs in sepia
grandmother's jade pendant	translucent white-green
Blemished sea-shapes	rise and dissipate
twist and untwist	speckles split
the coastline	Beyond waste chemicals
breaking stabilities	on the scaur
like phonetic entities	one pulse
through the murky field	alluvium birls
Listen	I want to hear you speak to me
I do not want the city	to forget you
or the other sailors	of Chinatown

The New Territories

When I first get off the plane, the heat hits me, tropical, alien. For once, I'm no different. Anonymity subdues me. This is where my past begins. I meet my uncle for steamed bamboo baskets of dim sum and oolong tea. He is tall, fair-skinned, almost like a *gweilo* people say. From my aunt's apartment windows I see tendrils of mist rise from Tai Mo Shan Mountain. Mammoth dragonflies hover, translucent-winged, their presence signalling the imminent fall of rain. I look for traces of my grandmother. A woman I meet, from the same village, mourns for her orphaned children, laments the tyrant husband, the cruelty of the mother-in law. She remembers my mother as a child. By day, I read the Tao Te Ching. I want to understand something about the nature of emptiness, to start again somehow. The character for Tao contains a head and a walking foot which means *the way*. In the Chi Lin nunnery on Diamond Hill there are lotus ponds, bonsai tea plants, purple and orange bougainvillea. Behind intricate screens nuns offer fruit and rice to Buddha. High-rise apartments loom over the skyline.

1961

The Valley Spirit never dies,
and is called Mysterious Female.
– Lao Tzu, Tao Te Ching

My aunt speaks in the dialect
of the Hakka tribe,
a language I do not fully understand.
Chinese gypsies, like dandelions,
flourish in adverse soil,
refuse to be trampled on,
the women's feet unbound.

She rises early in the morning,
a hollow bamboo reed
filled with amaranthine energy.
She puts on dark, loose trousers,
oriental blouse, a black–veiled hat.
She lights incense, replenishes the bowls of oranges
and white chrysanthemums on the ancestral altar.

We remember. We pray for our dead.
At night, we sit in her tiny room.
She tries to tell me what she saw –
1961, living in the same village
as my grandmother, in New Territories.
My grandmother, who one day drank weed killer
by the harbour at Sha Tau Gok.

The next day, we visit a temple
to honour the gods of literature and war.
Two banyan wishing trees stand in the courtyard,
their branches strewn with coloured streamers,
fluttering desires. There is fire in me again.
I feel her in my bones,
I hear her in the songs of birds.

Another Language

When I speak in Cantonese,
I'm a different person.
Louder, brighter.
The seven tones, ascending,
descending like musical notes.

My grandparents,
leaving the fragrant harbour
of Hong Kong, the Pearl River of Guangzhou,
for the dream of a better life in the West –
what did they make of English?

Alighting from the liner at the docks
in the rain, hearing Liverpool accents
for the first time –
two gold koi
swimming into the Mersey.

The Age of Innocence

My cousin, we share part of the same first name —
a Chinese pictogram of a cloud at sunset,
burning bright orange or violet-gold;
within it, the character for rain 雨.
How close we were, living almost as sisters.

I was six, you were eight. My father, the manager,
gone AWOL, mother weeping in the bathroom.
Empty afternoons, colouring pictures
on the dining tables, watching koi and angelfish
in a bright aquarium placed for feng-shui.

Today, at the same restaurant in a darkened
interior, with cups of jasmine tea, we stare
at the marsh — a hinterland on the coastline
of the Dee estuary. The sky opening up.
Hen harriers dive as merlins pursue.

Spring has brought skylarks weaving
their nests, golden samphire and scurvy-grass.
When we leave, I see that same flight of stairs
leading to another floor, a room we shouldn't
have entered all that time ago. We flew up

and down those stairs, trying to catch each other,
stop ourselves from falling. There was a bar,
a dancefloor, a silver glitter-ball. We dressed up
in my mother's clothes and stilettos, smeared lipstick
on rose-bud mouths, the line shifting around what we knew

and did not know. I wonder now if I lured you in,
if it was my fault we got lost —
I never was very good with directions.
They say that geishas inhabit another realm,
a flower and willow world. It's so cold.

Muse

I've tried endless entreaties,
offered green tea sweetened with rose and lily,
even dainty cups of osmanthus wine,

but none of this appeases. She shrugs her shoulders,
a real crazy-maker, slides down the banisters,
half-drunk mugs of mocha on window sills,

her Arabian perfume of amber and oud
rising out of books and magazines.
Twilight, she comes alive,

hips spiralling like fire.
In the morning she leaves.
She comes and goes as she pleases.

Why?

It happened because we were playing hide and seek.
It happened because we were in a wardrobe
because we happened to be there
because he happened to be there.
Because we didn't know exactly what was happening.
It happened because we were curious
because I wanted to be good.
It happened because mum had been crying
and you'd been staying up late
drinking whisky with your mates in the bar.
It happened because the wind howled in the backyard
and the mist covered over
the dark niches in the marsh
and sunsets astounded the sky.
It happened because you were in a bad head space
because the air was so still there
and we didn't make a sound.
It happened because you were chasing the big dream
to get rich quick
and it carried on happening
for a while at least
in his room
up the spiral staircase
while you were all downstairs.
It happened and I didn't know how to tell you
it happened when it did.

You Said

You said you'd seen me a few nights before
in *The Krazy House*. You were glad I'd come up
and spoken to you; our meeting was a kind of kismet.

On the dance-floor, you said you'd once
tried to stab yourself, and I didn't believe you.
Then you showed me a scar on your chest.

You said you'd call and you did – from a red
telephone box though the money ran out
before we said what we wanted to say.

You said your last girlfriend was called Rachel,
she ran off with some guy to Scotland, *a drip*, you said.
You'd really loved her. You said your brother was

schizophrenic, and looked like Elvis when he was fat.
Kant was your favourite thinker; you rated Plato
and Keats. Midnight on New Year's Eve,

we sauntered through Princes Avenue,
past the synagogue, the deserted Gothic church.
Fireworks ignited the indigo sky, revealing

the steeple, its pinnacles and broach spire.
We shimmied along the grassy strip and you said
you hoped someday there'd be no need for religion.

A friend of your sister's said you were very clever
but *not quite human*. When I told you, you laughed,
asked if that made you *super-human* and not to believe

a word they said. We were speeding as if
the air was chivvying us along, your arm
so tight around me all day, all night.

You said you'd drawn a black and white picture
of me the day after we met, that it even looked like me.
You said being with you gave me *a certain air.*

Now I think maybe it was the other way round.
Five years later, your mum says she'd wanted you
to leave this city, get away from that bedlam crowd.

She says you'd stepped in front of a train,
just a few days before – or was it after – her birthday.
It was January, white with cold. You weren't even thirty.

Last Night

I dreamt of you again
there in that Victorian house
draped with ivy and wisteria
by the lake and the park
an attic room overlooking
a garden gone wild
bramble   red clover   nettles

an array of sash windows
criss-crossed with bars
on the outside and inside
the frames dusty with cobwebs
a White-Witch moth

the room filled with smoke
and candlelight   perfume of juniper berries
no furniture   just a bed   an old turntable
a mélange of Rameau and Beefheart
cherubs on the ceiling
and up the alabaster walls

Black Star

He was everything I hadn't wished for.
He opened up, like foxgloves do, and sucked me in.
He was a name I couldn't say,
a train journey I shouldn't have gone on.

He was a crow crowing over me.
His smile was bulletproof, flashing six gold teeth.
His energy sang in the empty spaces he left
like the chimes of Buddhist bells.

A Certain Purity of Light

I.

Where was I?
    And what was I?
Standing in the umbra of your shadow.
Ensnared in your conjurings.
Forgetting my own magic.
I descended so deep
      into darkness, layers upon layers.
A cloud of not-knowing. I wandered in a fugue.
The sacristy of my mind overcame me
and I was truly lost.
The nigredo of your corvine heart fucked me up for ten years —
I should have heeded those spindrift voices
calling me to safety.

II.

My grandmother, whom I never knew,
how I miss you.
How and what were you?

I invoke your spirit,
make offerings
to the Three Mountain Kings.

III.

This October morning
is white
as it curdles its fury.

The light coruscates in the Georgian quarter.
I'm on Hope Street.
Before me, the Anglican cathedral looms.

IV.

On Huskisson Street
they say there's a ghost –
a man with no face.

Some nights
you can hear the ringing
of sword blades duelling.

V.

I had abandoned myself utterly;
I was a paper doll.
If you had held me up to the light,
it would have shone through.

VI.

Once, in your attic, I saw pieces
of the women you had loved
and who had loved you.

I saw a painting of a Christ-like figure,
his ribs like xylophones.
It was electric-blue.

There was a kimono
still wrapped in cellophane,
a discarded gift for someone else.

VII.

There is a certain purity of light
that arises
on these almost-winter days,
violet but not quite.

VIII.

Sometimes, there are nightmares still.
I wake up suddenly from a feeling
that I'm there again.
Trapped in that red attic room.

IX.

Now all I can do is laugh.
The dragon in me has returned.
The light of dusk quivers.
My flames blaze through the air.

Flower

Being here is hard because sometimes I don't want to be / Instead I want to be / as evanescent as a melody / just out of reach / fading into the background / fading into and out of you / like a wilting desperate violet / My violaine heart drips blood / oh my love / do you know how I feel / whenever I'm near you / within inches of your life / Drink me with your gaze / taste me now as I am / Sometimes I want not to be / the desire to be somewhere else / not to be present / my head or heart is in the past or the future / not stuck in linear time / in lineage as it is understood now / Sometimes I dream of elsewhere / let my fingers / your fingers / slant into spaces unseen / bring me back to life / before I cease to be

Going Home

I.

On this cobalt night, the fifteenth day of the eighth month,
the moon is a perfect circle, bone-white.
Look closely – that dark speck
on the surface is the moon-goddess Chang'e.

In ancient times there were ten suns
scorching the earth. The archer Houyi shot down
nine of them. The gods gifted him
two elixirs of immortality as a reward.

He hid them at home to take with his wife, Chang'e –
he did not want to be immortal without her.
Houyi went out hunting. His apprentice
Feng-Meng broke in, demanded the elixirs.

Chang'e refused. To elude him, she swallowed
the potions, then floated upwards into the sky,
her cloud-like robes flowing behind her.
She became air and light and sound.

II.

On such a night, Li Po dreamt of his home.
The harvest moonlight glimmered
in his room like frost on the ground.

Trying to capture the moon's reflection in a lake,
he died, one of the Eight Immortals
of the Wine Cup, just as you, my father,

always longed for your home on late nights
fuelled by whisky, *hieng-ha* – your village.
I wondered where this was, what China was like.

I listened to stories you told me – in Canton
you used to skip school to catch fish
in the stream. I remember the painting you had,

a Chinese junk sailing across a sunset harbour
to some unknown destination
and the picture from Hong Kong you gave me:

two pandas – a parent clasping its child
on a celadon background, bamboo, mountains
in the distance. To the side: black ink calligraphy.

III.

Father, on the fifteenth day of the eighth month
I returned. *And where is the heart?* I wonder,
as I retrace my steps to a grey Liverpool,
arriving home on the 80A bus down Rose Lane
that Saturday afternoon to find you slumped
in your leather armchair – a yellow fleece

caught over your head like a net.
A few weeks before, you had told me
you'd be able to travel the world,
among the sapphire rivers, pagodas,
jade mountains and lotus flowers of your youth.
I have been away so long, and you will be leaving soon.

Between Two Worlds

It was on Bridge Road in Mossley Hill,
where you can hear the rush of trains
passing by the backs of houses.
It was April and there were no lilies
in the room – not yet. There might have been tulips,
your favourite flower.
You were in your solitary, black leather armchair.
I think there was a bamboo plant
on the white desk, your little ornaments:
turtles for good luck, a tiny Buddha.

Outside, the sunlight was slowly dimming.
The street lights flickered on – a lurid, amber glow.
You were slipping in and out of consciousness,
no longer wild-eyed from morphine.
When your breathing changed,
my sister phoned the nurse.
Then we helped you to your bed,
my sister and I on either side.

The Tibetans say that at the time of death,
the blood in the centre of the heart forms three drops,
the external breath ceases and, engulfed by blackness,
we become unconscious.
We swoon into blissfulness.
Awareness dissolves into inner radiance
at the centre of the heart
like the meeting of mother and child.

Outside your window
we could hear the extractor fan
whirring relentlessly,
the banging of an iron wok,
customers placing their orders;
the TV blaring in the background,
the sound of laughter,
my mother and brother carrying on the family business.

A Prayer for My Grandmother

Mother, let us enfold our griefs in lotus leaves,
cast them in the vagaries of the river,
let its alchemy bloom the most enchanting flower
in the murkiest of waters.

Let us admit how ghosts
can resurrect themselves,
become our holy guardians
who watch over us as we sleep.

Mother, let us remember how our women
were once warriors, unbeholden to any man,
how the world was not made by a god
but a goddess who created the earth from mud.

She held up the sky with the legs of a giant tortoise
allowing every star to shine its light,
the sun to burst forth, the lovely moon to come out at night.
Let us remember that grandmother's name means *spring beauty*.

Swallows

The morning after our elopement,
on the balcony of our hotel room
you point to the eaves of the roof
where a tiny swallows' nest is tucked away.

They flicker out, almost fish-like;
the Mediterranean glitters in the sunlight –
little black birds! We watch them
as they embrace the Cypriot sky in twos and threes.

In oracle bone inscriptions, the character
for a swallow 燕 shows its open mouth,
forked tail, wings unfolded. Bearers of good fortune,
symbols of spring, they bring prosperity

by making the old new again; their mud nests
repair the cracks of walls and graves.
British swallows spend winter in South Africa,
soar through Western France, the Pyrenees,

down Eastern Spain into Morocco, across the Sahara.
The distances they dart and dance, radiant with light
and darkness, the journeys they traverse and risk.
Before departing on a journey, a sailor would tattoo

a swallow on his chest, hands or neck.
When he returned to his home port,
he would get a second tattoo. If he drowned,
the swallows would carry his soul to heaven.

The Meaning of Names

Your surname comes from the Old English word
lēah for a meadow or forest clearing –

your love is an airy space which holds me
in both light and shade.

At our wedding banquet, my mother wrote
our surnames in gold on firecracker-red paper

with the symbol for double happiness 囍,
rejoiced at how your English name –

the character for a plum tree 李 –
sounded the same as her mother's.

Legend says that a minister's son
of your name escaped with his mother

from the cruelty of an emperor
and survived by eating plums.

I'm loath to relinquish my surname 徐,
which tells me how I want us

to live our lives together, *slowly*, *gently*,
my name which came from my father

and grandfather – an immigrant who carried it
on his lengthy crossing, anglicised it

unrecognisably to what it sounds like in essence,
a breath. Their marble headstones

have two sets of names, as will mine.

Love Token

after Andrés Cerpa

If anything, I'm a witchy vagrant locked inside
an endless hall of mirrors, patterns and repetitions,
wandering. I've often been in the wrong place at
the wrong time, my wasted youth traded for a
ghostly ride in a fairground, crazy merry-go-
round music haunting my memories. Family,
friends, ancestors and spirits: light a candle when
I'm gone, so the pretty moths can come closer to
the flame but not be burnt. I don't want to go,
just yet. The moon is so elegant tonight. All week
long shit storms and hailstones raged. Thank you
for the damned and wild beauty you have given
me here, though most days I couldn't find the
words to tell you, the way a Chopin nocturne
plays inside my head every time I think of you.
It remains unknown. I smash through the glass.
I leave you the key.

Acknowledgements

Grateful acknowledgments to the editors of the following journals where earlier versions of some of these poems were first published: *Ambit, Oxford Poetry, The Rialto, SMOKE, Soundings, Wild Court.*

A number of these poems appeared in *Ten: Poets of the New Generation* (Bloodaxe, 2017) edited by Karen McCarthy Woolf. Thank you to Karen for editing my poems during this process.

'Another Language' was a runner-up in the Bi'an 2018 Writing Awards for Poetry.

Epigraph is taken from Emily Dickinson's poem 536 in *Emily Dickinson: The Complete Poems* edited by Thomas H. Johnson (Faber & Faber, 1975).

Thank you to Helena Nelson and John Glenday for their helpful feedback on some of these poems.

Many thanks to individuals and organisations who have encouraged and supported my creative and critical work: Nathalie Teitler and The Complete Works, Mary Cooper and Bi'an, Sandeep Parmar, Sarah Howe and the Ledbury Emerging Poetry Critics scheme, Dave Ward and The Windows Project.

Special thanks to Mimi Khalvati for her wonderful mentorship on The Complete Works.

Thank you to everyone at **ignition**press for believing in this pamphlet, particularly to Alan Buckley for his meticulous reading and editorial work.

Most of all, thank you to my family and friends, with love, especially my mum and Chris.

FSC
www.fsc.org

MIX

Paper from
responsible sources

FSC® C015185